MOCHA

A loyal and loving cat…

Written by Dana Russell
Illustrated by Anna Herzlinger Kogan

Copyright © 2019 Dana Russell
All rights reserved
ISBN-13: 9781794488953

"Some people say the most loving pets are the ones that choose you."

Mocha's timeline
1998-I'm with my original family.
2001-I meet Nick and Dana.
2003-It's just Dana and me.
2011-Freddie comes inside and changes everything.
2013-We say, "Goodbye."

My name is Mocha. This is my story.

I moved into this house in Portland, Oregon with my family after we moved to the West Coast from Maryland. After a few years, we moved to another neighborhood in the city.

I really missed my old house, so I ran back. It was about 30 blocks away so I had to dodge a lot of cars, people, and dogs along the way.

I was happy to be back in my neighborhood, but MY house was empty. The neighbors, Mark and Sue, saw me and called my family who came to pick me up and take me away. This made me very sad.

When we got back to the new house, I had to stay inside for a week to make sure I wouldn't run away again. But, I had other plans.

As soon as I saw an opportunity, I escaped and ran back those 30 blocks for a second time! Something was pulling me back to MY house and neighborhood, which I needed to patrol.

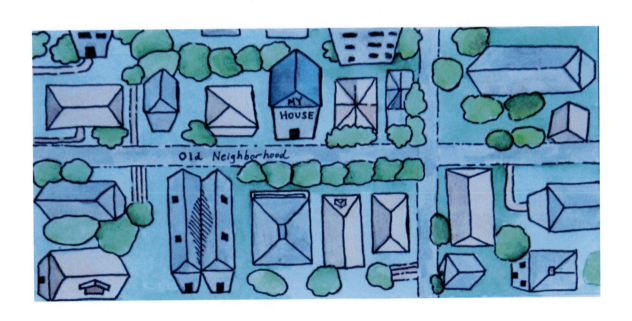

MY house was still empty when I arrived and I couldn't get in! I was tired, hungry, and dirty. A nice lady around the corner, Nancy, fed me while I stood guard at MY house.

Some time later, two people showed up and walked in MY house. I tried to get in when they opened the door.

This couple had no clue who I was nor how important I would become. Plus, they didn't realize this was MY house!

I became friends with these humans called Nick and Dana. They thought it was strange I gave up my family for this house and neighborhood. Luckily, they kept me since the family was going to take me to the pound (whatever that was) because I kept running away. No one understood the reason why I kept coming back, but one day they'd figure it out.

I liked Nick a lot. He would play chase with me outside and laugh at my antics. Dana loved hearing this sound from the kitchen window while watching us. It took quite a while before they'd let me in the house, but once they did all I had to do was bang on the screen door and they'd open it. Then I could go in and out as much as I wanted.

Sometimes, I'd lay on their bed even though I wasn't supposed to do that. At first Nick said firmly, "No way is Mocha going to be on our bed!" I won him over though and often Dana would hear Nick talking to me as I rolled around on the bed. I knew how to get what I wanted with my persuasive ways. Dana used to say often, "Mocha is the smartest cat I've ever met." I think she was right.

Life was so happy for me with Nick and Dana. They gave me nicknames like Mocha Sue, Fluffy Buns, and Wiggleworm, since I'd scoot on my side along the bed like a worm. It was pretty cute, if I do say so myself. Mostly though, they called me Mocha and loved me a lot.

One day, Nick got really sick. It wasn't like him to miss work. He got worse and Dana drove him somewhere. I wondered where he went and I started to have a bad feeling, like something was wrong. I hardly saw anyone for days and was lonely for my people.

I never saw Nick again. People started coming in and out of MY house and Dana was crying, as were all these other people. I began to realize why I had left my original family and felt the need to be back at MY house. With Nick gone, I needed to be here to take care of Dana.

People stayed with us for a while and then it was just Dana and me. She wasn't the same-no smiles, no laughter, very quiet. This is what humans call grief. Nick had died unexpectedly and we both missed him terribly.

When Dana would go down to the basement and sit and cry on the ground near Nick's drums, I would always lick her. She would always reach over, pet me, and tell me, "I love you Mocha Sue."

Sometimes, I got into big trouble on purpose to take Dana's mind off her sadness since she had to focus just on me.
-I got locked in the abandoned house across the street.
-I got trapped in a garage for 24 hours.
-I cut my paw on accident and she had to take me to the vet for stitches!
-I pulled a tablecloth out from under drinks and food while her friend was over causing things to go flying. It was actually quite a funny move on my part.

Often, Dana would sit in the garden where she and Nick had planted vegetables. She watched the progress of Nick's pumpkin (Halloween had been his favorite holiday). I'd come and keep her company.

Finally, Dana went back to work as a teacher. While I worried about her during the day, I went back to patrolling the neighborhood. Each day around the time I knew she came home, I made sure to be on the porch waiting. If I wasn't there, she went wandering the neighborhood looking for me. I was happy at night when it was just the two of us.

Dana always tried to pick me up, but I was not one of those cuddly cats that liked to be held. I'd protest loudly with a hiss! I did love Dana though. She was MY person. I made sure to sleep right by her side every single night.

Days, weeks, months, and years passed. Slowly, Dana re-entered life. At one point, Dana made me an indoor cat. I thought I'd hate being stuck inside, but I adapted pretty well and Dana liked knowing I was somewhere inside the house instead of roaming and defending my territory in the neighborhood getting into mischief.

After several years indoor as the Queen, Dana showed me something through the window. Way out on the grass there seemed to be a cat sleeping. If I'd been outside, I would have definitely chased him off MY property!

Dana started going in and out of the back door an awful lot. I'd hear her talking to that cat, whom she started calling Freddie. I wasn't worried about her spending time with him since I knew she'd never bring him in. I'd heard her tell her friends that I would go "absolutely crazy" if another cat came in. Therefore, I knew my rule as Queen was secure.

Then, all of a sudden one day, she brought Freddie in! He was locked in the downstairs bathroom and I stuck my paws under the door to try and get at him. From what I could tell, he'd been hurt so he was inside temporarily. Dana made sure to keep us apart...for now.

Freddie got better and she kept feeding him outside. One day she said, "Mocha, I need to bring Freddie inside for good. The raccoons outside won't leave him alone. Can you let him live inside with us?"

I couldn't believe what she was saying! Mocha Sue Fluffy Buns Wiggleworm Russell was NOT a cat that accepted others into her territory. I was a one person cat and would have to show this boy cat who was in charge!

I still remember when she opened the door to let him in. Freddie sauntered in and went right past me looking for food. I completely froze, though I'd planned on swatting him immediately. What was going on with me?

It took us a while to adapt to each other. I made sure to let Freddie know that this was MY house first and that Dana was MY person. When she'd lie on the couch, I got to lie on her lap. At night, I slept next to her and he had to sleep by her feet.

Over time, we actually became good friends and would take turns "meowing" in the morning to wake Dana up. It almost sounded like we were singing. She would wake up and often laugh seeing and hearing us. This made us happy!

Dana fed us in separate rooms because Freddie was such a pig! He would always run to try and eat my food. I often let him because, I guess, I loved him even though I still swatted at him sometimes to remind him who was in charge.

One Sunday morning after Freddie and I had been friends for several years, Dana came downstairs and I was walking funny, my head was tilted, and my pupils were really big. She grabbed me and took me to an emergency vet since something was wrong.

The vet took me away and did some tests. She tried shining a light directly in my eyes, but it didn't bother me.

The vet brought me back in the room with Dana. I was very upset and irritated. The vet told Dana that I had a stroke, I was blind, and I had other medical issues going on. They talked for a while about a lot of things and I paced back and forth very uncomfortable and angry in my new dark world.

Finally, Dana and I went in another room. She was holding me (I actually let her) and telling me how much she loved me. We had been together over 12 years by now. I had a feeling she was saying "goodbye." I knew I'd done what I needed to do. I came back to MY house all those years ago for a reason--to take care of Dana after Nick died. I knew she'd be okay because Freddie would take care of her now. I let go of worrying about her in that moment, and I slowly drifted off to an endless sleep.

About the Author

As an elementary teacher for the past 26 years, Dana Russell has always loved the impact literature can have on people. After losing Nick and realizing the important role Mocha played in her grief process, she set a goal to write a children's book to help those going through a difficult time.

Dana is a native Californian who grew up in SoCal, but now lives in the Bay Area, after moving away to Oregon for 15 years, where Mocha and Freddie entered her life. Family, friends, animals, running, baking, travel, and "enjoying each moment" are what make Dana happiest. She hopes you too have the unconditional love of a pet in life at some point, and if not, there are many animals out there ready for adoption.

About the Illustrator

Anna Herzlinger Kogan lives in California, but she is a Jersey girl at heart. She is an artist and has taught art at the middle school and elementary levels for 20 years, where her students amaze her every day with their art and creativity.

She enjoys painting and photography, and gains inspiration from California's beautiful scenery. It has been a dream of Anna's to illustrate a children's book.

She would like to thank her husband and two sons who always support her art and provide valuable feedback. She would also like to thank her parents who always encouraged her to follow her passions.

Made in the USA
Lexington, KY
17 December 2019